Vale of Dears

cartoons by
Joe Lane

published by About Comics, Camarillo, California

Vale of Dears
Originally published by Michael Book Co., 1958
About Comics edition published April, 2018

Customized editions available

Send all queries to *questions@aboutcomics.com*

"Ooh—Eee—Ooh—Ah-Ah—
Ting Tang Walla Walla Bing Bang—"

"Take my advice, Sister, stay single!"

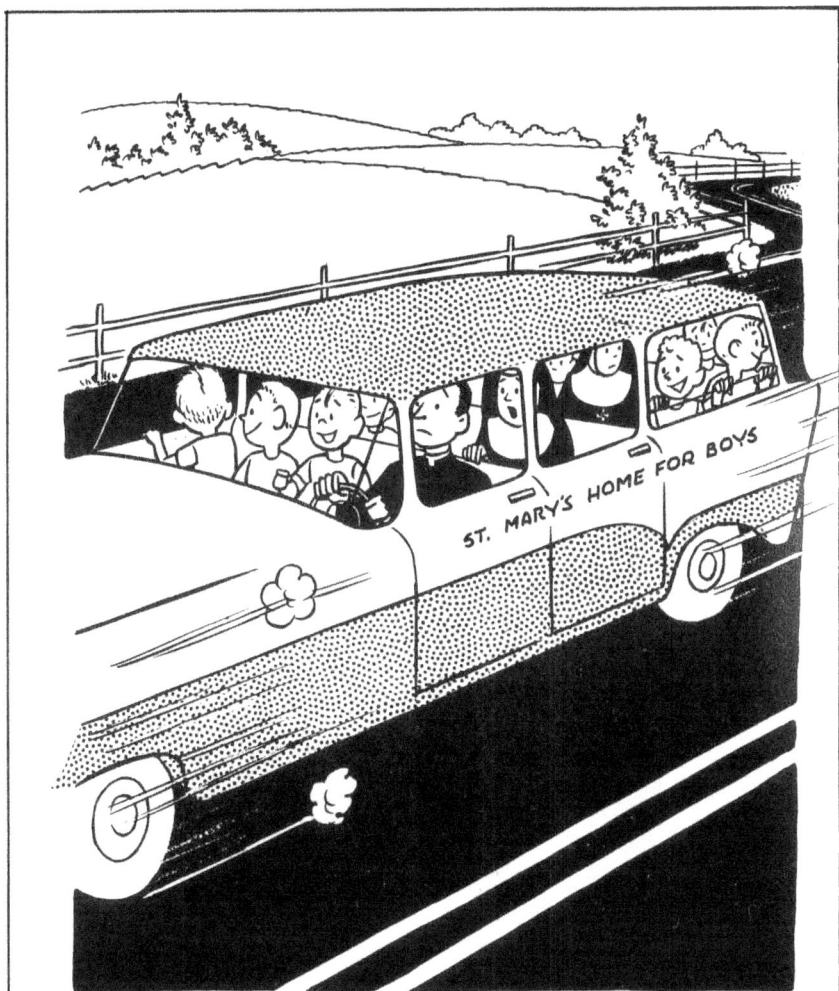

"*Not too fast now, Father, be careful—*
Look out—Slow down—"

*"We usually say, 'An error has been made',
not, 'Somebody goofed'!"*

"Sister Mary Dorothea spent quite some time
on the islands!"

"And may I say, Sister Mercita, in all my travels I've never seen a better job of camouflage on hash than yours!"

KEEP OFF NEWLY SEEDED

"Is there also a Mickey Mouse cartoon?"

"Now that, Sister Cordella,
is what I call encouraging a vocation!"

"And if he's naughty, Sister Humilissa,
you have our permission to spank him!"

"Oh, dear—this happens every time I have to back up!"

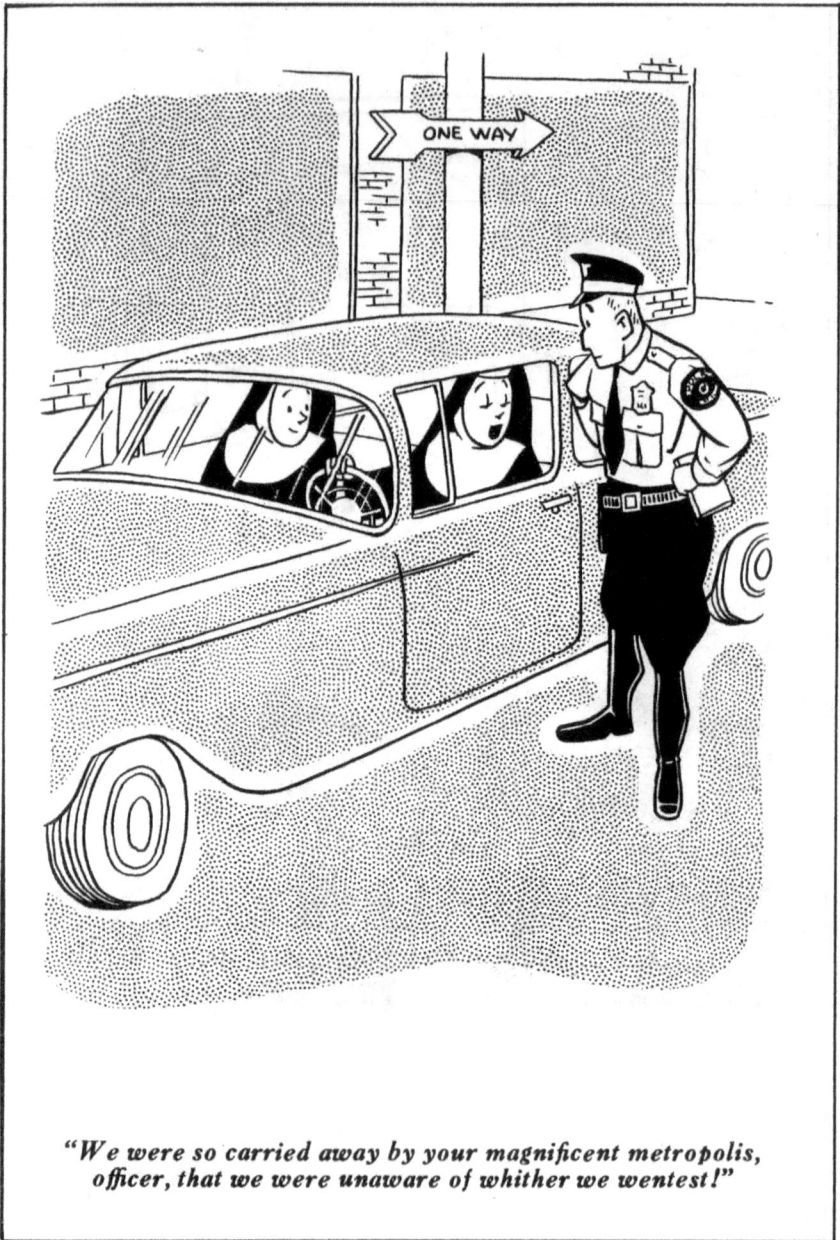

"We were so carried away by your magnificent metropolis, officer, that we were unaware of whither we wentest!"

THROUGH THESE
PORTALS PASS THE
MOST BEAUTIFUL
GIRLS IN THE WORLD

"It's an expression that was quite popular in my day."

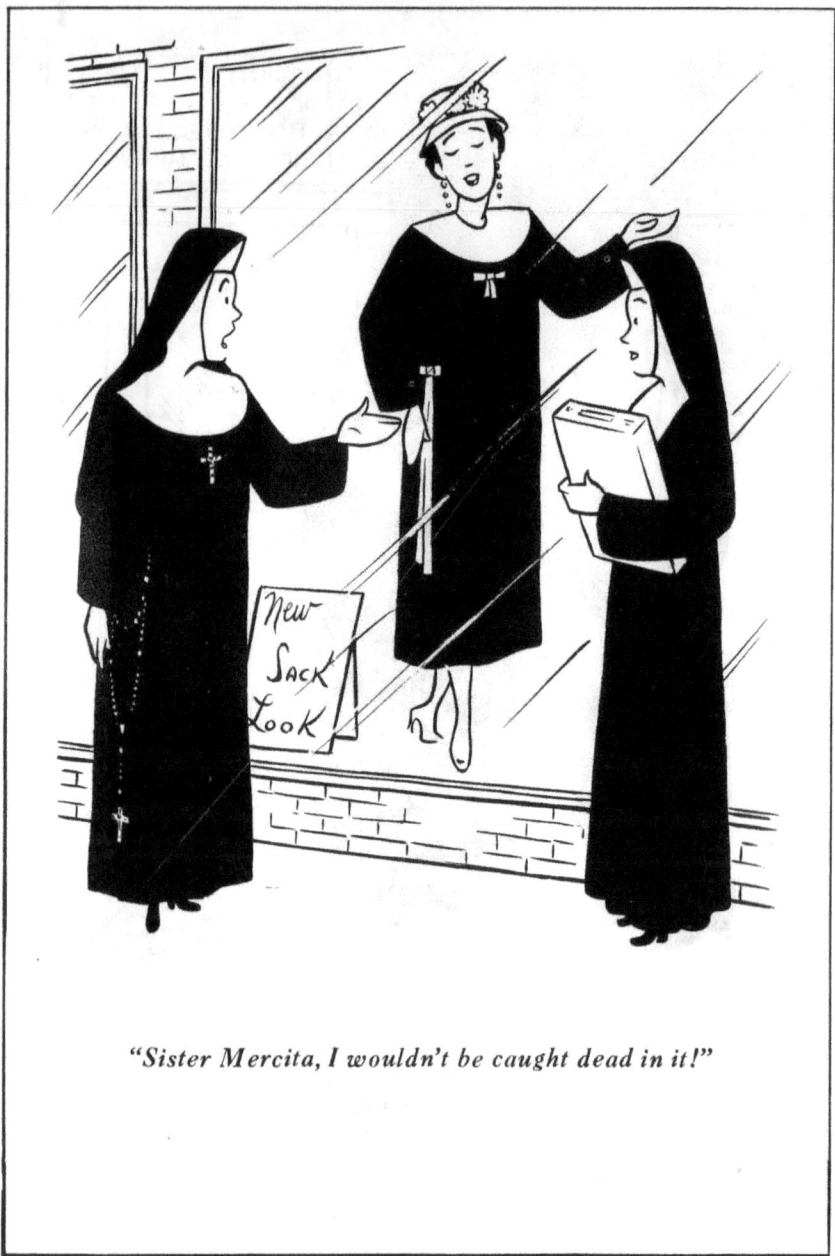

"Sister Mercita, I wouldn't be caught dead in it!"

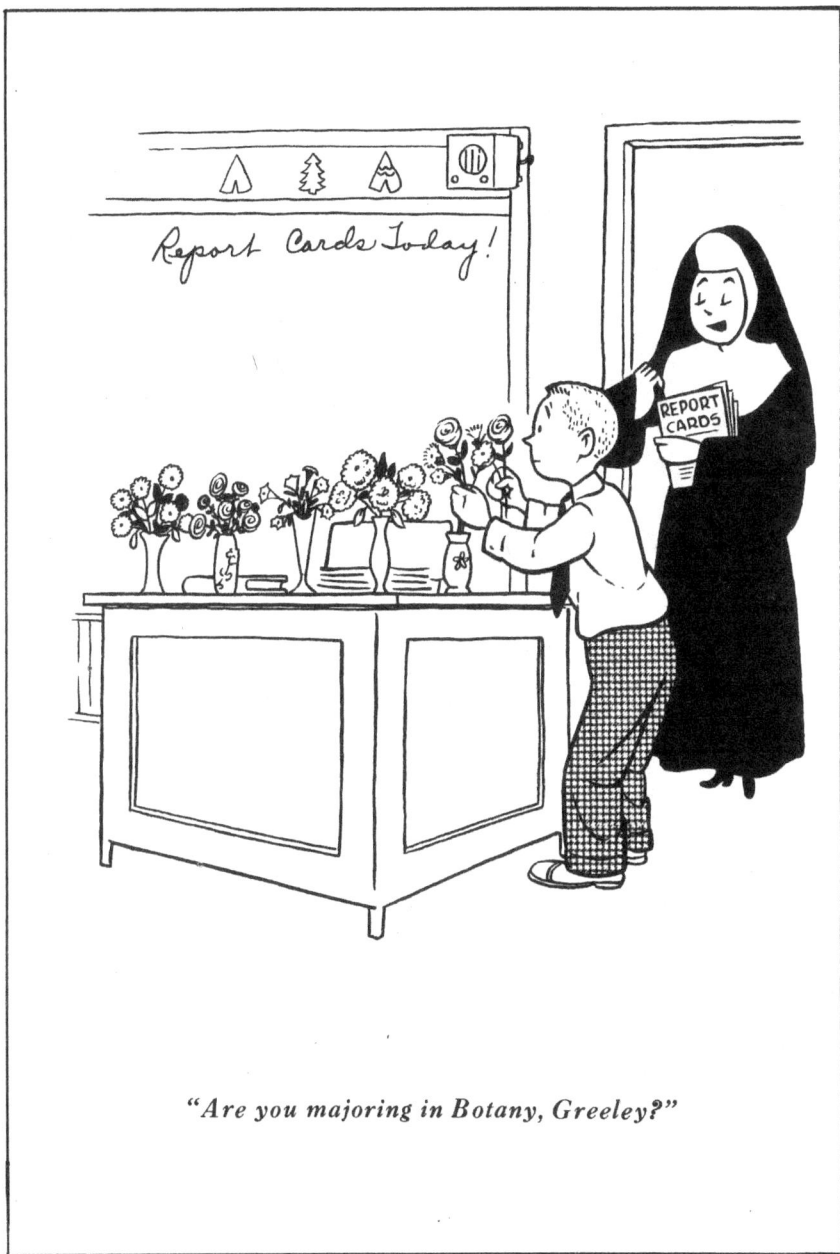

"*Are you majoring in Botany, Greeley?*"

"Who turned off the Notre Dame game?"

"Here's my note for being absent, Sister Mary Sulpice!"

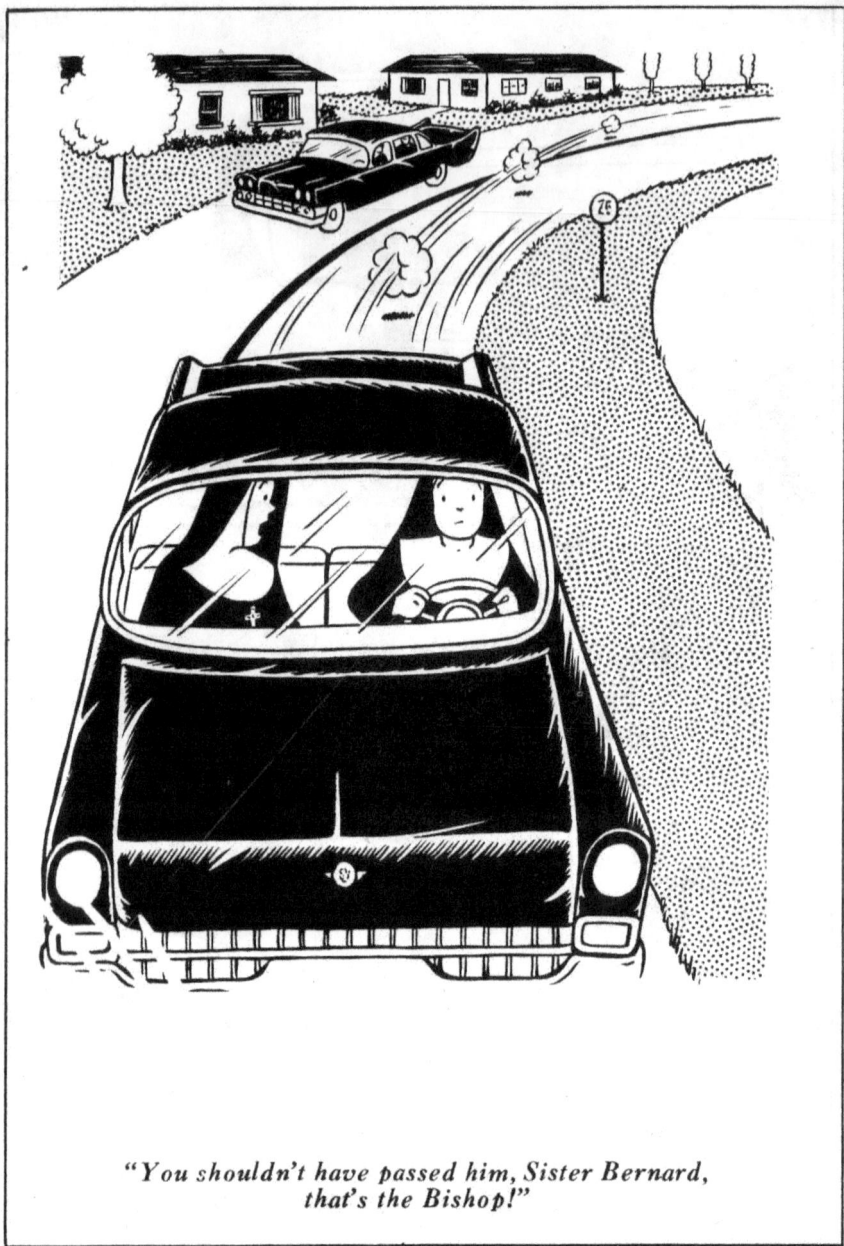

"You shouldn't have passed him, Sister Bernard, that's the Bishop!"

"To make a long story short, Sister Ivana, nyet!"

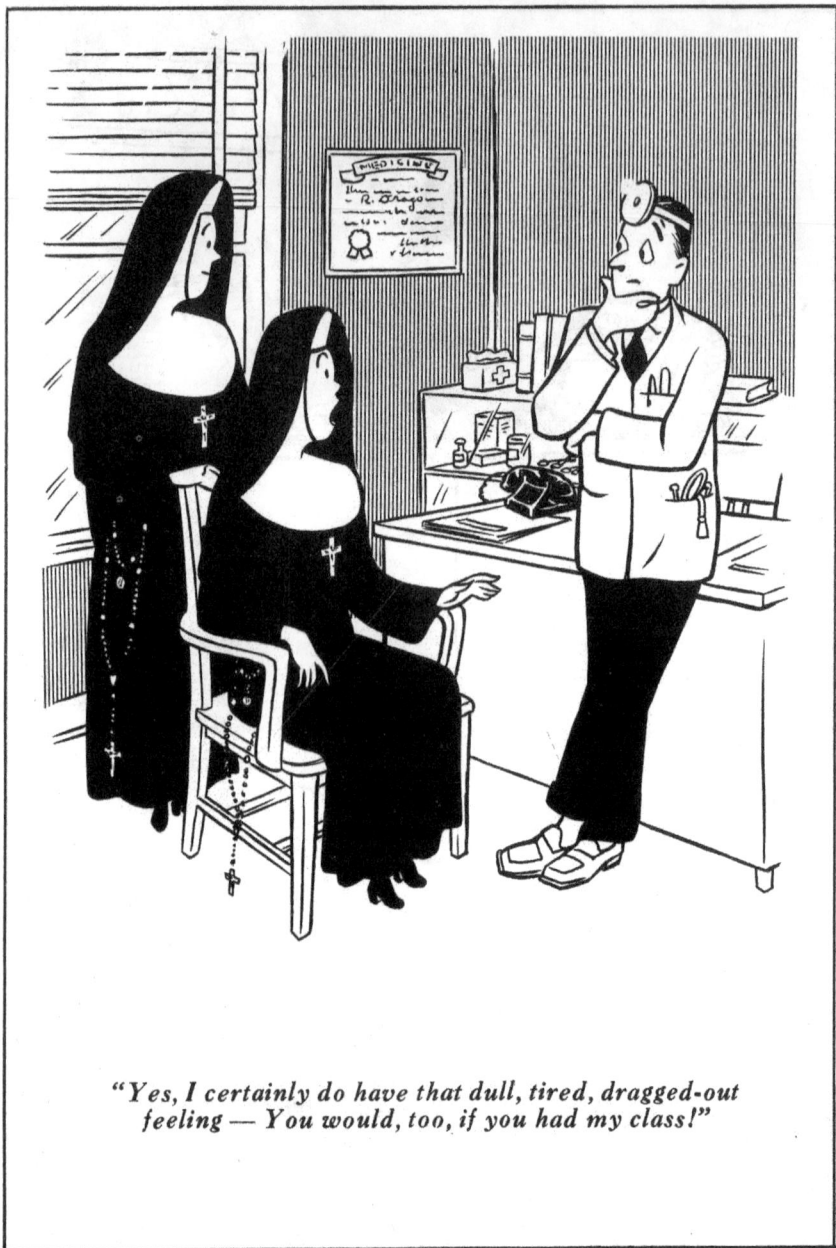

"Yes, I certainly do have that dull, tired, dragged-out feeling — You would, too, if you had my class!"

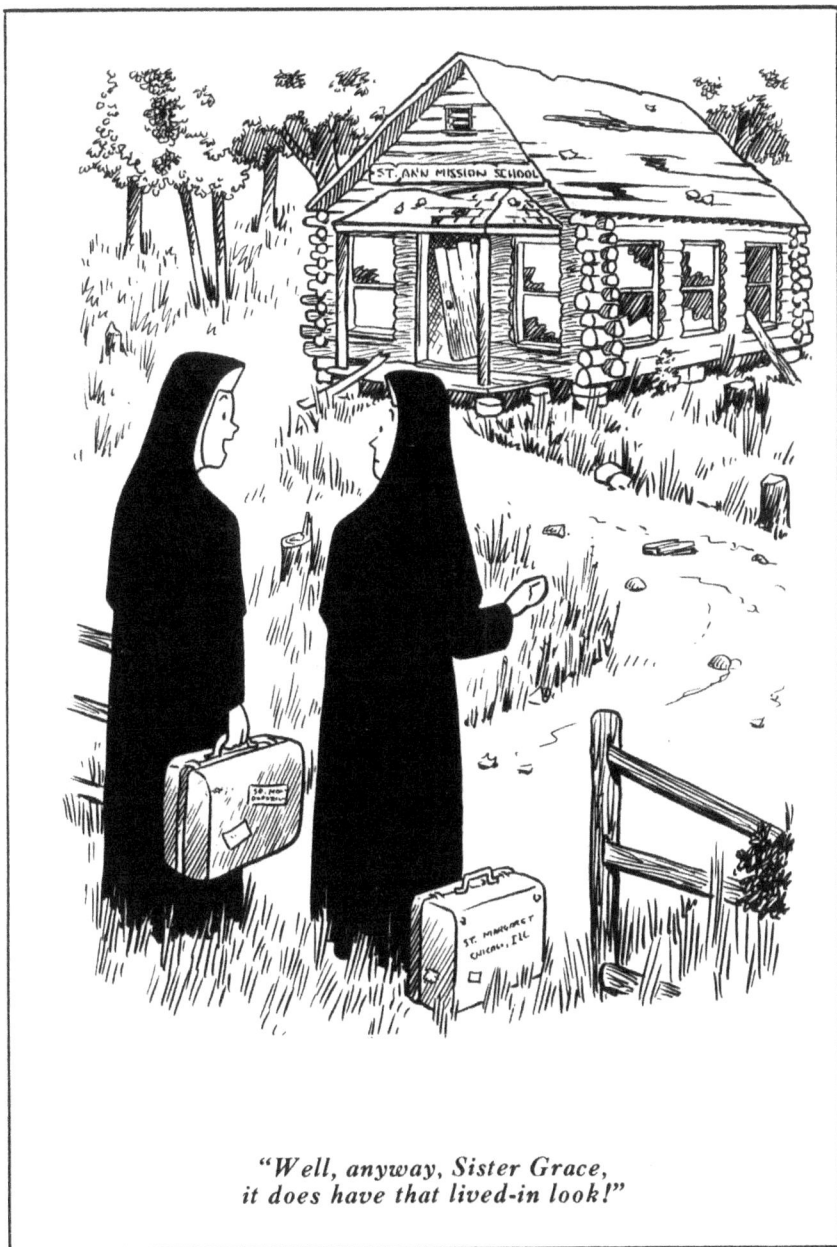

"Well, anyway, Sister Grace,
it does have that lived-in look!"

"Up here, Sister Henrica, we use the large missal for our night prayers."

"I wish, Sister Patricia Anne, we could AFFORD all the economy sizes!"

ST. GABRIEL
CONVENT

"Sometimes, Miss Daly, it helps if you imagine this as a part of your purgatory!"

"Sorry Im late, Sister Agnesine, but I couldn't get more than 19,000 miles per hour out of my rocket ship!"

"Here is your latest nuptial blessing!"

*"Care to join me in a Novena
to get transferred back into the jungles?"*

"It's her first day in high school, Sister Ellarose.
She's a little shy!"

"*Remember, Lucifer, love thy neighbor!*"

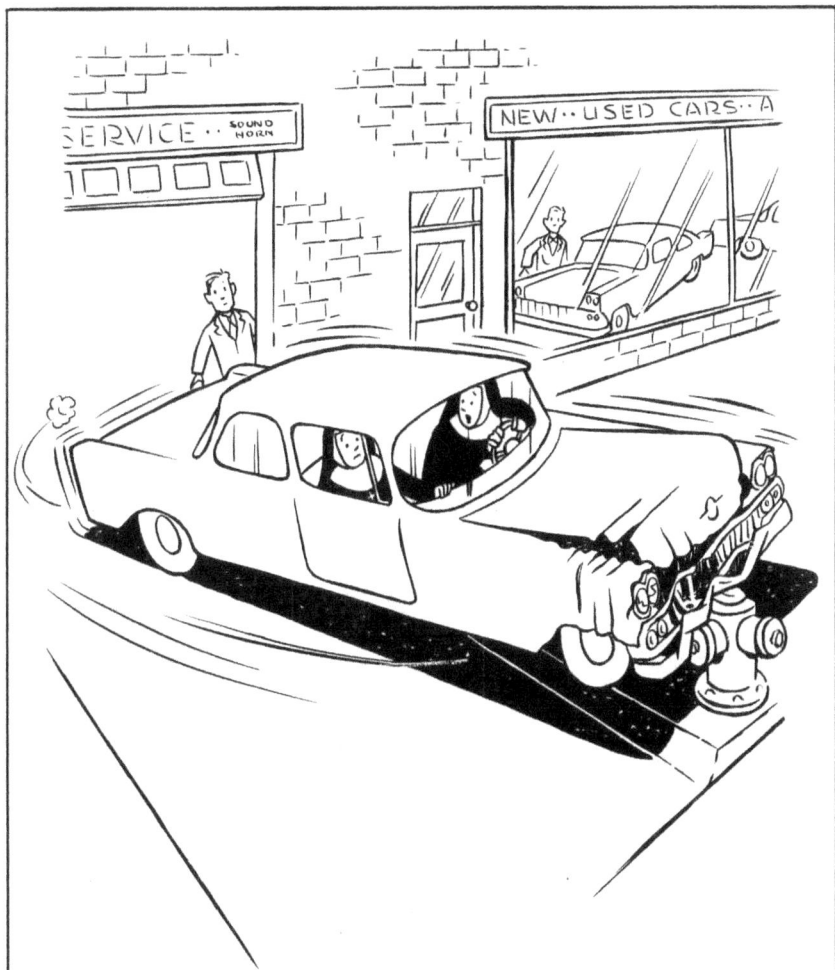

"Well, Sister Matthias,
that takes care of the 'breaking in' period!"

"Sandra Glamure—why, she used to be in my class as Mathilda with the runny nose!"

"Well, Doolittle, what's the excuse this time?"

"Baseball, anyone?"

"How about $50.00 cash
and the balance in trading stamps?"

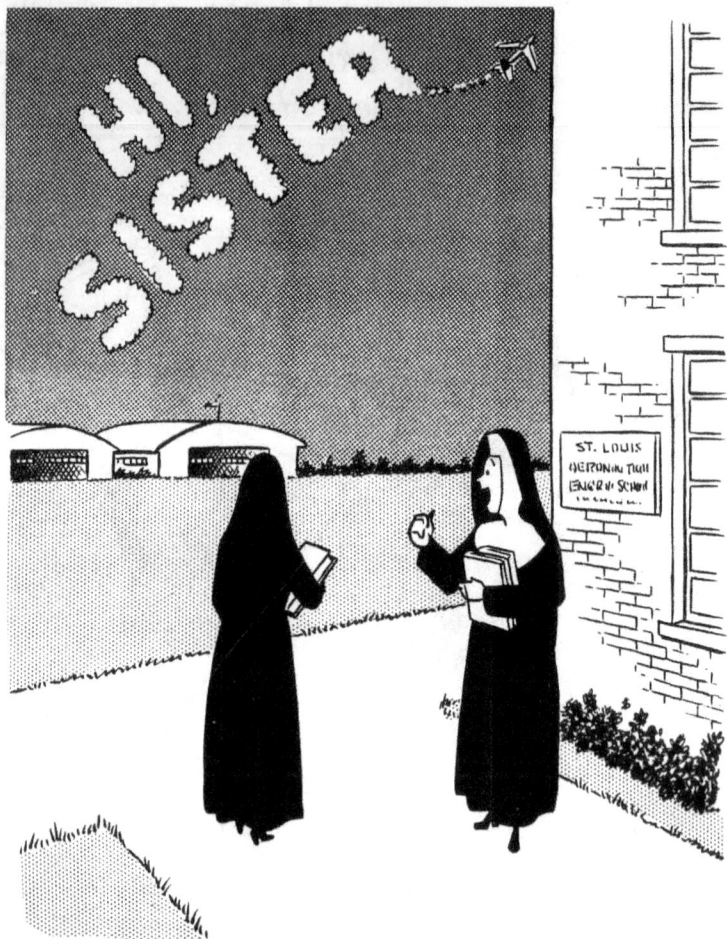

"That's Willie, Sister—
He always used to scribble on the blackboard!"

"The class is very proud of Morrison, Sister Patrick, he made his first 70 today."

"Oscar likes onion sandwiches."

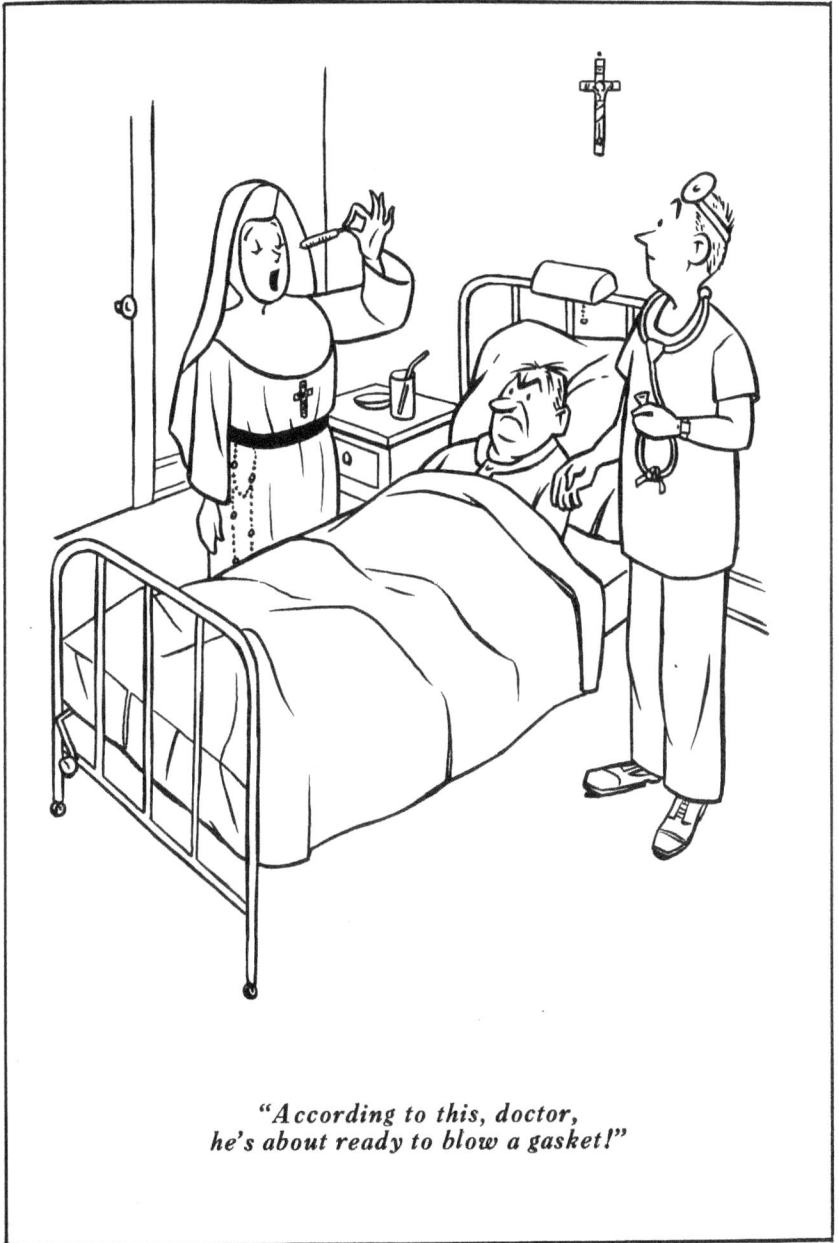

"According to this, doctor,
he's about ready to blow a gasket!"

"And this, Sister Benedicta,
we use in case of a heavy dew!"

"Look, Sister Willene, one of God's little——

—creatures."

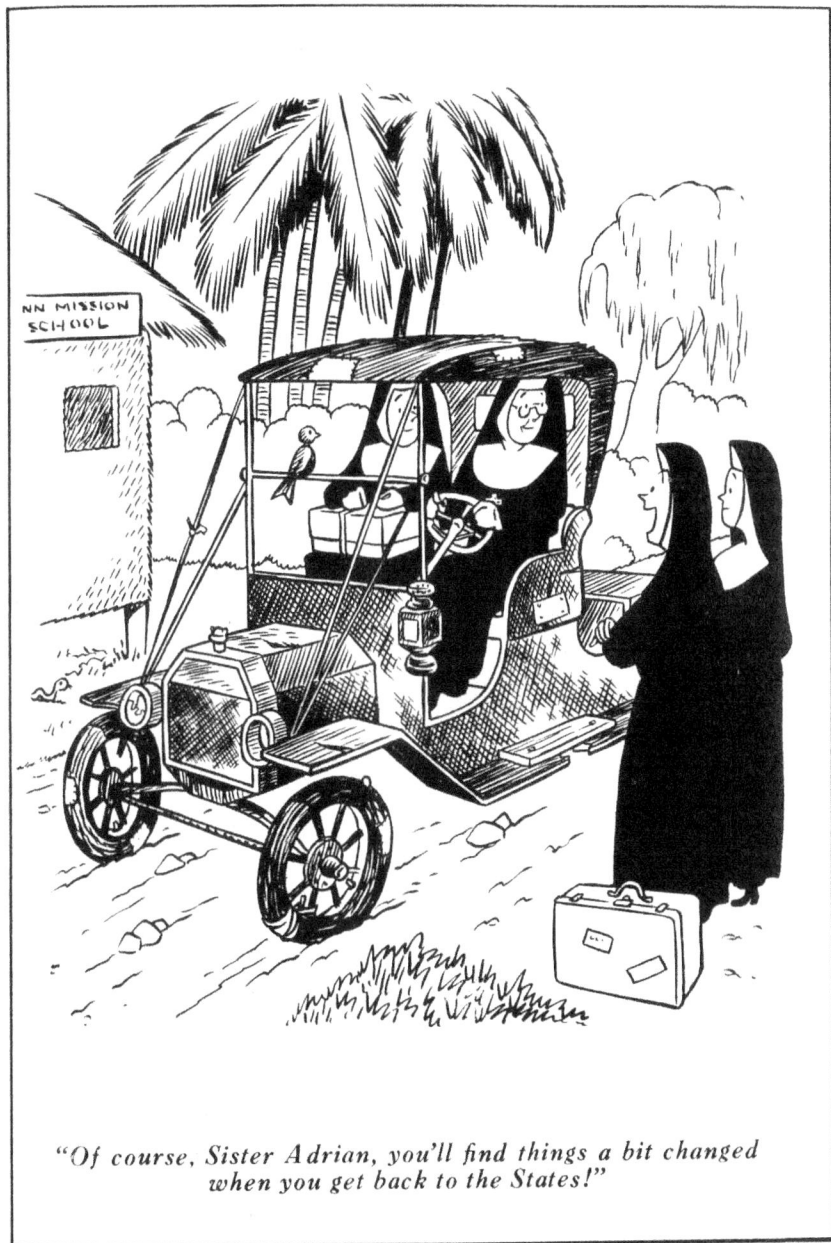

"Of course, Sister Adrian, you'll find things a bit changed
when you get back to the States!"

"Would you save us your cancelled stamps?"

"Oh, it's lovely, Sister Mary Adelgond,
but give me the old coal and wood stove."

"Before we begin, class, may I say this will be a do-it-yourself test, and I DO mean, do it yourself!"

"*Come on, all you wranglers, the Chuck Wagon's ready!*"

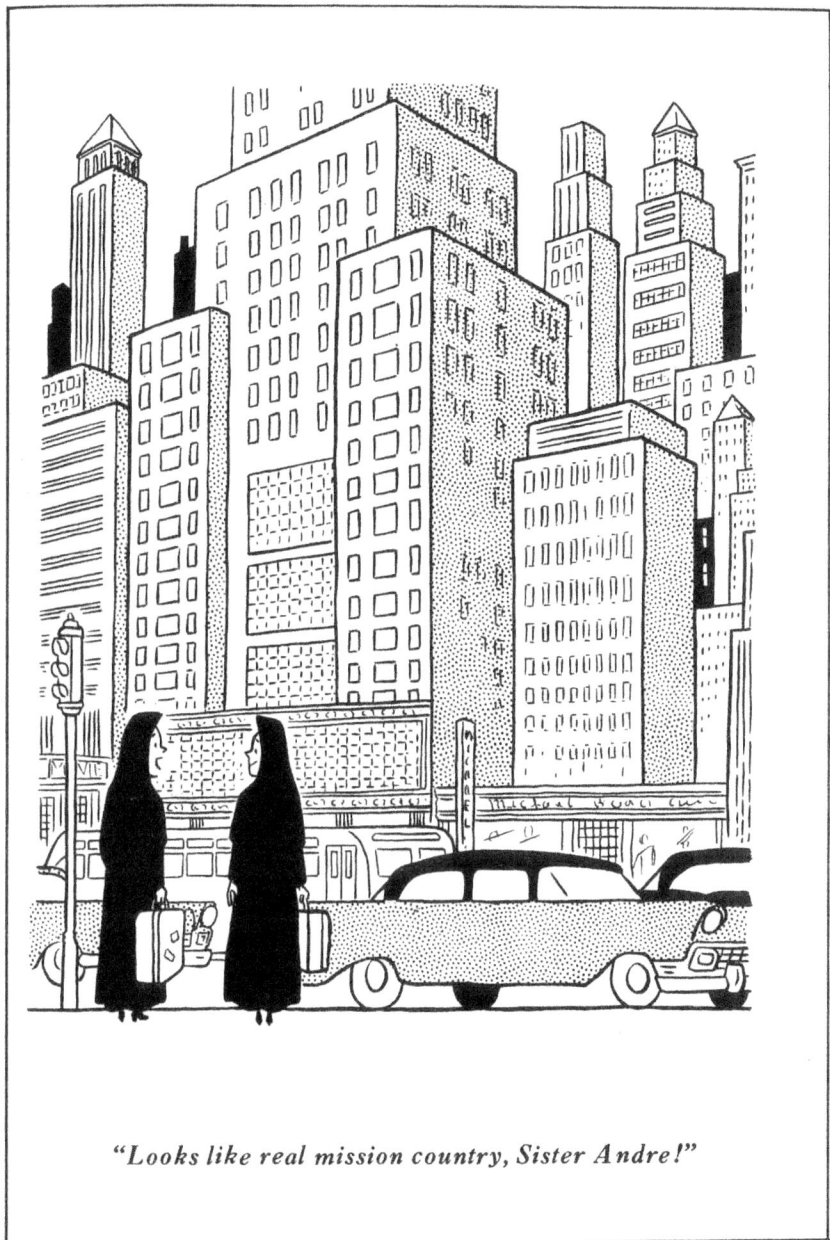

"Looks like real mission country, Sister Andre!"

"We'll have to start another novena for funds,
Sister Mary Bilhild. Our creditors demand payment!"

"*Even with pay-TV, Sister Thomas More,
we use our set just as much as before!*"

"I like home to be neat and tidy."

"Outer space is nothing new to Thaddeus—he's been staring into it for the past semester and a half!"

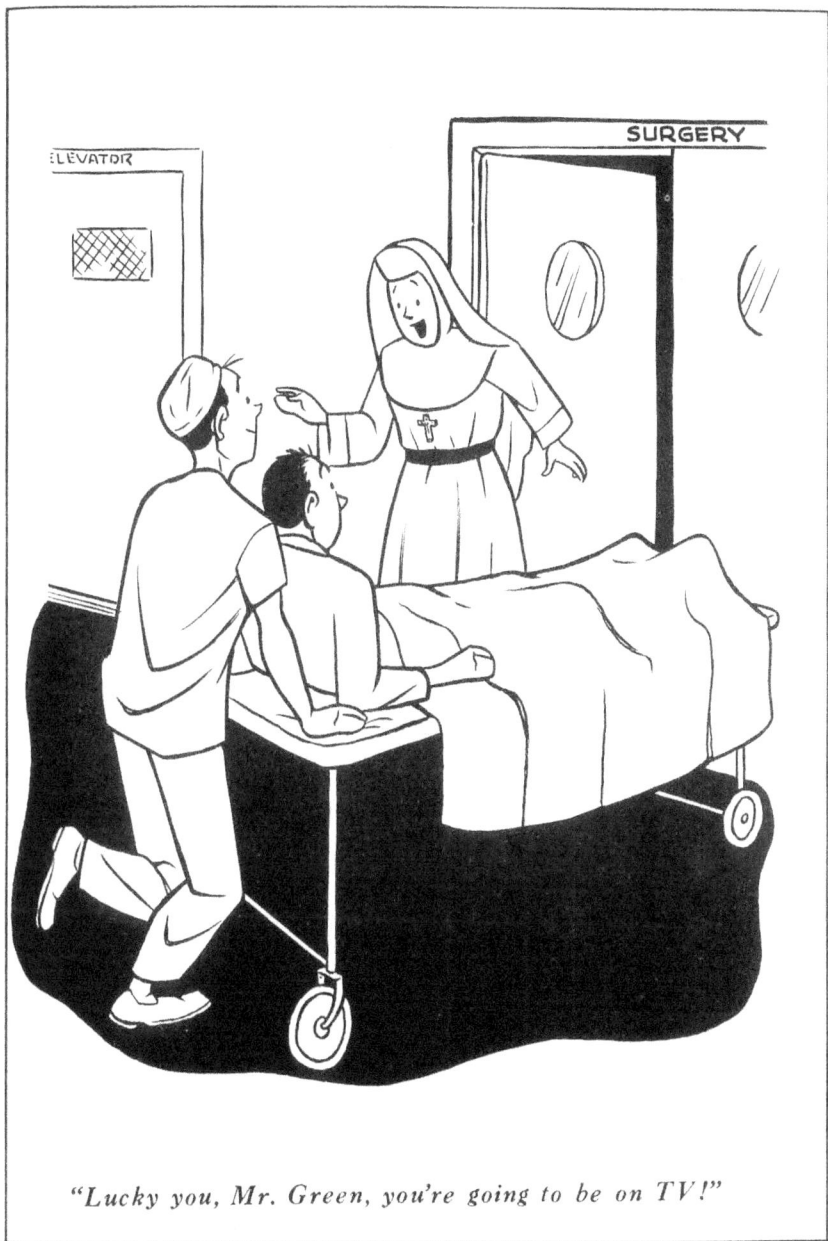

"Lucky you, Mr. Green, you're going to be on TV!"

"Do you suppose it would be all right,
Sister Madeline Marie? I hear it's made by monks!"

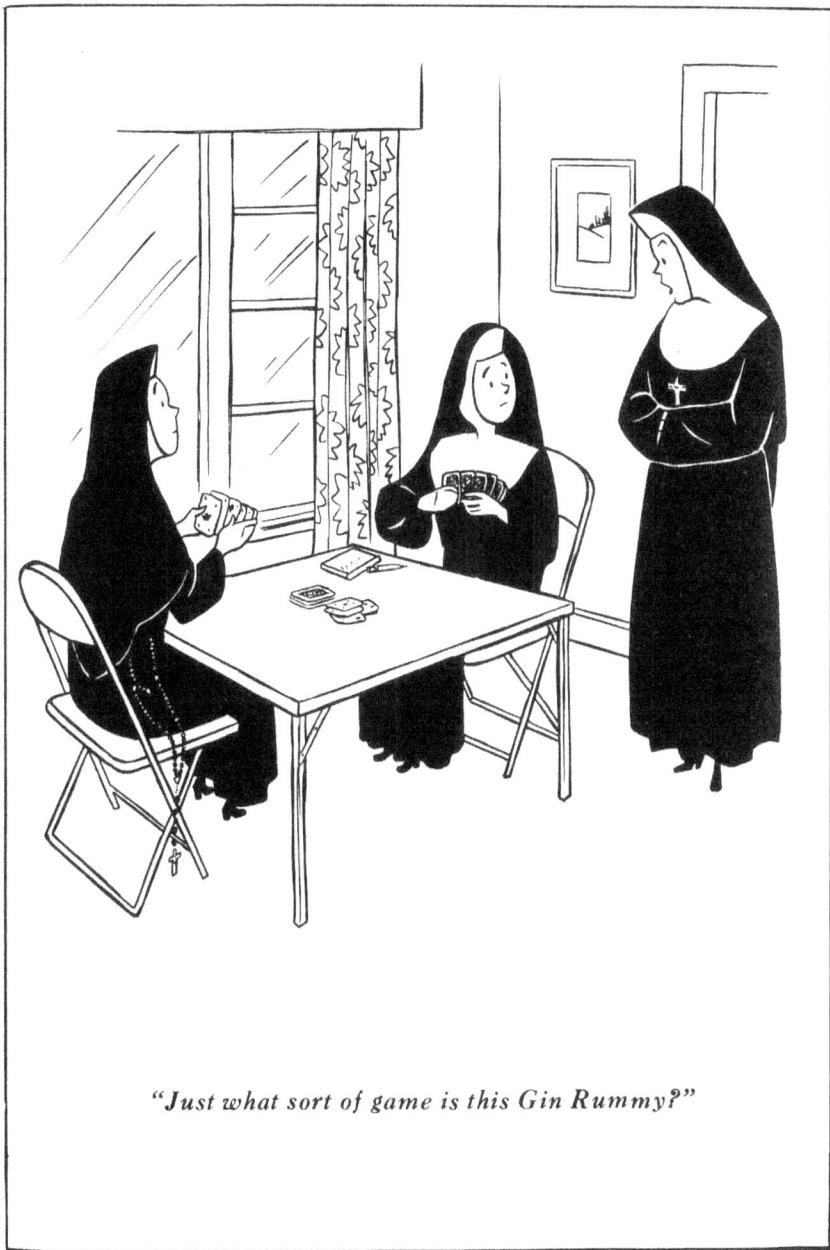

"Just what sort of game is this Gin Rummy?"

"It must be a treat for you Sisters to get outside the convent walls once in a while!"

"*At home, Sister Louisine, we simply ignore him!*"

"But, Sister Imelda Marie, we're not permitted to visit!"

"*Take me to your leader!*"

"Well, outside of his school work,
Eddie is one of my smartest pupils!"

Get all our little books of Joe Lane's little nuns

Our Little Nuns
More Little Nuns
Nuns So Lovable
Vale of Dears
Yes, Sister! No, Sister!

or get

The Big Book of Nun Cartoons
a lifetime supply all in one volume!

Look for them where you got this book,
or visit www.AboutComics.com

Classic Cartoon Collections!

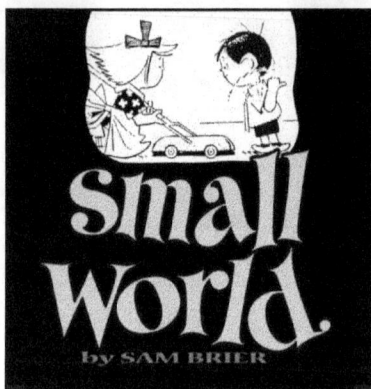

Sam Brier's 1950s quirky comic strip is about kids playing as adults... or adults drawn as kids.

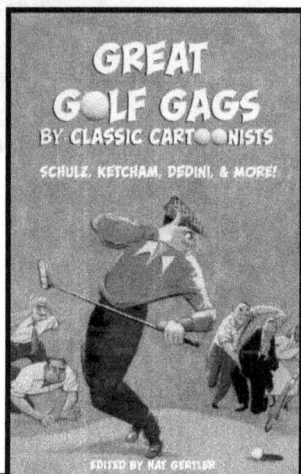

Golf cartoons by Hank Ketcham, Eldon Dedini, Virgil Partch, Bill O'Malley, & more

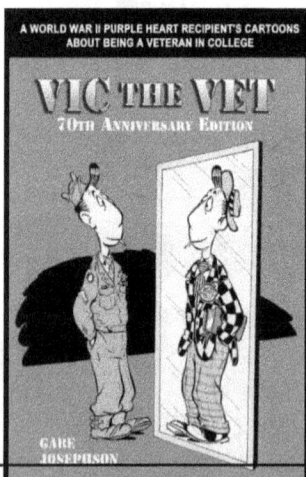

Cartoons about being a World War II vet at college on the GI Bill... by a World War II vet while at college.

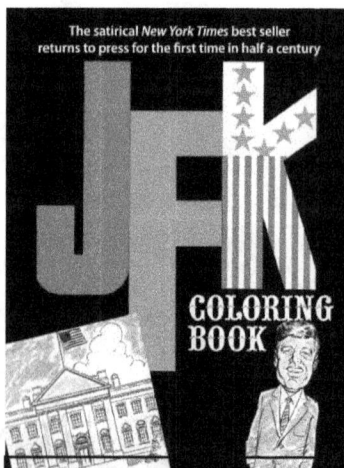

Mort Drucker illustrates this New York Times best-seller